The Good Fight

TED STAUNTON
JOSH ROSEN

Scholastic Canada Ltd.

Toronto New York London Auckland Sydney
Mexico City New Delhi Hong Kong Buenos Aires

*To Margaret, and in loving memory of my parents and grandparents,
who lived those years and shared their stories.*
—T.S.

*To Sarah, for all the support. And to my family,
for raising me with a sense of history.*
— J.R.

Scholastic Canada Ltd.
604 King Street West, Toronto, Ontario M5V 1E1, Canada

Scholastic Inc.
557 Broadway, New York, NY 10012, USA

Scholastic Australia Pty Limited
PO Box 579, Gosford, NSW 2250, Australia

Scholastic New Zealand Limited
Private Bag 94407, Botany, Manukau 2163, New Zealand

Scholastic Children's Books
Euston House, 24 Eversholt Street, London NW1 1DB, UK

www.scholastic.ca

While events described and some of the characters in this book may be based on
actual historical events and real people, this graphic novel is a work of fiction.

Library and Archives Canada Cataloguing in Publication
Title: The good fight / Ted Staunton, Josh Rosen.
Names: Staunton, Ted, 1956- author. | Rosen, Josh (Illustrator), illustrator.
Identifiers: Canadiana 20200367498 | ISBN 9781443163835 (softcover)
Subjects: LCSH: Antisemitism—Ontario—Toronto—History—20th century—Comic books,
strips, etc. | LCSH: Antisemitism—Ontario—Toronto—History—20th century—Juvenile fiction.
| LCSH: Jews—Ontario—Toronto—Social conditions—20th century—Comic books, strips, etc.
| LCSH: Jews—Ontario—Toronto—Social conditions—20th century—Juvenile fiction. | LCSH:
Immigrants—Ontario—Toronto—Social conditions—20th century—Comic books, strips, etc.
| LCSH: Immigrants—Ontario—Toronto—Social conditions—20th century—Juvenile fiction.
| LCSH: Toronto (Ont.)—Race relations—History—20th century—Comic books, strips, etc.
| LCSH: Toronto (Ont.)—Race relations—History—20th century—Juvenile fiction.
| LCSH: Toronto (Ont.)—Ethnic relations—History—20th century—Comic books, strips, etc.
| LCSH: Toronto (Ont.)—Ethnic relations—History—20th century—Juvenile fiction.
| LCGFT: Historical comics. | LCGFT: Graphic novels.
Classification: LCC PN6733.S73 G66 2021 | DDC j741.5/971—dc23

6 5 4 3 2 1   Printed in China 62   21 22 23 24 25

Author's Note

My grandpa, W. J. Stewart, CBE, was mayor of Toronto when the riot at Christie Pits happened. He never talked about it to me; I was young when he died, in 1969. Later, when I learned the story, I wanted to share it, and a bit of his. This book is the result.

The Good Fight takes you back in time to a younger, very different city and country, growing and changing into the one you know today. Some people don't like change. Sometimes they resist it in ugly ways.

Some of the things you'll find in this story will be hard to witness. They were hard to write. Some of the language the characters use is hateful. But pretending it didn't happen would be worse. And in the end, this is also a story about those among us who stood up against hatred, for fairness and justice.

August 16, 1933, was a pivotal moment for Canada. It made us face the future, whether some chose to look then or not. More than ever, the time to look — and hear the story again — is now. I think Grandpa would agree.

~ Ted Staunton

Chapter 1

Duke Man

TORONTO, AUGUST 1933

BEACHES...

BOARDWALKS...

BREADLINES...

...BROKEN HEADS.

A *WHIZ MOB* LIKES A CROWD, BUT NOT THAT KIND.

BALL GAMES. THAT WAS *OUR* KIND OF CROWD.

TOMMY HAD TOLD US A BALL GAME WAS A *SWELL PLACE* TO PICK POCKETS.

YOU READY?

AS I'LL EVER BE.

TOMMY WAS OUTSIDE HI'S BILLIARDS. IT WAS A TEST RUN. HE'D TAUGHT US LIKE HIS UNCLE TAUGHT HIM.

YOU HAD TO KNOW THE MOVES TO MAKE IT WORK. IT HAD ITS OWN LINGO TOO. THE GUY TOMMY CHOSE WAS THE *MARK*.

PLUG WAS THE *STALL MAN*. HIS JOB: DISTRACTION.

♪

ACH! WATCH IT, JUNIOR!

WHOOPS!

4

TOMMY WAS THE *MECHANIC*. WHILE PLUG STALLED THE MARK, TOMMY WOULD PICK HIS POCKET...

...AND HAND OFF TO ME AS I PASSED.

THAT MADE ME *DUKE MAN*, BECAUSE THE MONEY ENDED UP IN MY DUKES.

IF IT WAS THE REAL DEAL, WE'D ALL KEEP MOVING IN DIFFERENT DIRECTIONS. THIS TIME...

OKAY, SID!

HERE, *SUCKER*!

WHAT? WHY YOU LITTLE--

JUST A *GAG*, MAXIE! CAN'T YA TAKE A *JOKE?*

STAY ON THE SOUTH SIDE. OUR TURF.

GEEZ, TOMMY, WE'RE NOT STUPID.

ENEMY TERRITORY...

CHRISTIE PITS!

THAT WAS WHAT EVERYONE CALLED WILLOWVALE PARK. ALL THE CITY BALL TEAMS PLAYED THERE. IT WAS A CRACKERJACK PLACE TO WATCH A GAME...IF YOU WERE CAREFUL.

WATCH OUT FOR THE PIT GANG.

WHATSA MATTER, GIRLIES? SCARED? THEY DON'T LIKE JEWS AND ITALIANS IN THIS NECK O' THE WOODS, DO THEY?

LUCKY FOR ME, I'M IRISH!

EVERYONE IN OUR NEIGHBOURHOOD KNEW TOMMY'S REAL NAME WAS TADEUSZ LEPOFSKY. HE WASN'T THE FIRST TO CHANGE HIS NAME.

WE RAN A COUPLE OF GOOD PLAYS IN THE PARK.

I HAVE TO ADMIT IT: IT FELT STRANGE TO HAVE MONEY IN MY POCKET.

HEY! YOU'RE NOT FROM AROUND HERE!

NO MEATBALLS ON OUR TURF!

AND NO YIDS EITHER! GET OUTTA HERE.

WE'RE GOING, WE'RE GOING!

OKAY, ONE MORE. SPREAD OUT.

TOMMY PICKED A MARK.

OOPS!

HEY! WATCH IT!

♪

IT WAS LIKE TURNING A SWEET DOUBLE PLAY...

...EXCEPT THIS ONE WENT SOUR.

OW!

STRIKE ONE!

NOT SO FAST, TWERP!

RRR!

STRIKE TWO!

CRASH!

YER OUT!

BLOODY IDIOT!

WE MET UP AT TOMMY'S HIDEAWAY.

TWO FOR ME, ONE FER EACHA YOUSE.

BUT--

LISTEN, KLEIN, THAT'S THE DEAL! I'M THE OLDEST, I TAKE ALL THE RISK. NOW WHADJA GOT?

IT WAS ONLY THEN I SAW WHAT STUCK ME.

14

MAYBE I'LL COME BY LATER, BUY SOME HOOCH OFF THAT MOONSHINER DAD OF YOURS.

HE'S *NOT* A MOONSHINER!

ONLY BECAUSE NO ONE WOULD BUY THAT *ROTGUT* HE MAKES.

HOME AGAIN!

BACK TO LOSE SOME MORE, SHRIMP?

HE DON'T EVEN KNOW WHERE HIS *OWN* FATHER IS.

GEEZ, WE GOTTA MAKE MONEY ANOTHER WAY.

WHO'S GONNA HIRE US? HALF THE WORLD IS OUT OF WORK, AND--

JEWS AND ITALIANS DON'T GET HIRED.

YOU MEAN YIDS AND WOPS...

HYMIES AND MEATBALLS...

KIKES AND DAGOS...

HA! IS THAT THE BEST THEY CAN DO?

WE'RE SMARTER THAN THEY LOOK!

THAT'S WHY WE GOTTA TRY MY PLAN.

OKAY, BUT FIRST WE TAKE SOME OF THIS AND SELL PAPERS TOMORROW.

NOW, TELL ME A JOKE.

HORSE GOES INTO A BAR. BARTENDER SAYS, WHY THE LONG FACE?

READ A GREAT NEW BOOK...

...TIRED OF IT ALL, BY *ANITA COFFEE.*

CIAO, PAPA. CIAO, MAMMA.

WE WENT TO THE *BALL GAME.*

WHO WON?

WE DIDN'T STICK AROUND.

BEFORE THAT WE HAWKED THE AFTERNOON PAPERS. *THE TELEGRAM.*

THAT *RAG?* MAKE ANYTHING?

I GOT IT HERE. DID *GREAT!*

HI, SID.

HI, ROSIE.

OH, YOU CUT YOURSELF.

HOW DID YOU SELL PAPERS WITHOUT GETTING DIRTY HANDS?

I...WELL...

CLICK!

SID, YOUR POP IS UPSTAIRS.

POP AND I RENTED A ROOM FROM THE VENDITELLIS IN THE HOUSE THEY RENTED.

IT WAS ALL WE NEEDED. AND THEY NEEDED THE MONEY BAD.

POP AND ANGELO HAD BEEN IN THE WAR TOGETHER.

NOW POP WORKED AS A CLOTHES PRESSER AT LUXE GARMENT.

NONNA V. CARED FOR ME AFTER MA AND SARAH DIED FROM THE INFLUENZA.

YOU'RE BACK.

SOLD SOME PAPERS. *THE STAR*. MADE FIFTEEN CENTS.

FEH, YOU'D DO BETTER READING UP FOR NEXT YEAR. GET AHEAD, SCHOOL STARTS SOON.

POP, YOU KNOW I DON'T NEED SENIOR FOURTH.

I'M THIRTEEN, OLD ENOUGH TO GET A JOB, HELP--

DOING WHAT? THERE IS NO WORK UNLESS YOU'RE EDUCATED.

I COULDN'T EVEN GET YOU INTO LUXE, INTO THE SHMATTE TRADE WITH ME. AND YOU'RE NOT ENDING UP THERE. EIGHT DOLLARS A WEEK IF YOU'RE LUCKY!

BUT WE NEED--

WE GET BY. YOU GET EDUCATED. END OF THE STORY.

WHERE'D YOU GET *THIS*?

FOUND IT. WE WENT BY THE BALL GAME AT THE PITS.

NAZI TRASH. IT'S THOSE PUNKS FROM BALMY BEACH. THEY WANT JEWS OFF *THEIR* BOARDWALK. IT WAS IN THE PAPERS.

YOU EVER READ THOSE PAPERS YOU SELL?

SURE...

NOW THAT BASTARD HITLER RUNS GERMANY, THERE'LL BE MORE OF THIS.

STAY CLEAR OF THAT BOARDWALK--AND CHRISTIE PITS, TOO. THEY HATE US THERE.

AND TOSS THAT FILTH DOWN THE JAKES. IT'S NOT TO BE IN OUR HOUSE.

WE DON'T HAVE A HOUSE...

I'M GOING OUT FOR A WHILE.

WHERE?

FRIENDS. MIGHT BE LATE. READ A BOOK, HUH?

APART FROM ANGELO, POP HAD NO FRIENDS I KNEW OF. HE WASN'T A KIBITZER.

I COULDN'T SQUARE POP'S *FRIENDS.* WHO WERE THEY?

THERE WAS ONLY ONE WAY TO FIND OUT.

...MMWMN...
MM...MWM

MM...N...ERS...
ASSOC--

GET OUTTA
HERE, KID. JUST
SHOOTING CRAPS.

THANKS. BE SEEING YOU.

ACH!

'SCUSE. SORRY, BUD.

MOONSHINE WASN'T JUST IN THE SKY THAT NIGHT.

IT'S A
HOT NIGHT.

YEAH,
G'NIGHT.

Chapter
2
Strike Out

POP AND TERESA BOTH WORKED AT THE LUXE GARMENT FACTORY ON SPADINA, EIGHT TO SIX, FIFTY HOURS A WEEK.

NEXT MORNING, PLUG AND I WERE OUT BEFORE EITHER OF THEM, WHILE THE AIR WAS STILL COOL.

HOW MANY?

UH, TEN?

TEN CENTS.

WHADJA GET?

MAIL AND EMPIRE. SELL 'EM TWO CENTS APIECE. IT'S *EASY*. COME ON!

BOARDWALK--

BALMY--

LATEST BALL SCORES!

MAYOR CALLS--

HEY!

I *TOLD* YOU TO GET *LOST!*

OOF!

WANTA *TRY?*

An ominous cloud of race tension gathered as swastika emblems were flaunted on the east-end boardwalk last night by members of a rapidly growing club, despite Mayor Stewart's warning that anti-Jewish behaviour will not be tolerated. The mayor now calls for--

GERMAN UNREST!
Berlin (AP) Over the last ten days, harassment of Jews by Nazi storm troopers has led to the attempted exodus of thousands, in the belief that a merciless pogrom is being unleashed--

HOW'D YOU DO?

LOUSY. YOU?

JUST *ONE LEFT*. LET'S GET SOME BREAKFAST.

WE WALKED HOME THROUGH KENSINGTON. IT WAS ALREADY HEATING UP.

THE STORE...

PLUG AND ROSIE'S NONNO VENDITELLI CAME TO CANADA. HE STARTED OUT COLLECTING SCRAP TO RE-SELL.

RAGS, BONES, BOTTLES!

HE GOT A PUSHCART...

...THEN THE STORE.

VENDITELLI

FRUIT + GOODS

WHEN WE WERE LITTLE, WE USED TO PLAY IN THE BACK.

THEN THINGS WENT SOUTH.

NONNA V. DIED.

ANGELO WAS BADLY HURT.

NONNO V. HAD A HEART ATTACK.

TERESA TRIED TO RUN THE STORE. BUT NONNO V. HAD GIVEN TOO MUCH CREDIT. WHEN HARD TIMES HIT, NO ONE COULD PAY.

THEY LOST EVERYTHING, EVEN THEIR HOME.

CLOSED

THAT'S WHEN WE THREW IN TO RENT WITH THEM.

C'MON, TELL ME A JOKE. HOW *HOT* IS IT?

IT'S SO HOT HENS ARE LAYING *FRIED* EGGS.

ON AUGUSTA AVENUE, THE BAILIFFS WERE EVICTING A FAMILY WHO COULDN'T MAKE THEIR RENT.

I'M GOING TO MAKE A MILLION DOLLARS IF IT KILLS ME.

YOU AND ME BOTH, BROTHER.

THEN WE TRY *MY* WAY TONIGHT. WE'RE READY.

AW, PLUG, I'M NOT--

YOU LIKE *TOMMY'S* WAY BETTER?

AWRIGHT.

'*GIORNO*, NONNO. I BROUGHT YOU THE PAPERS.

DID YOU MAKE ANYTHING?

EIGHTEEN CENTS.

I NEED IT FOR SHOPPING. MAMMA LEFT A LIST.

PAPA WANTS THINGS TOO, AND YOU HAVE TO HELP WITH THE WAGON. HE'LL TELL YOU.

I NEED *BREAKFAST* FIRST.

TWENTY POUNDS POTATOES, TEN POUNDS WHITE SUGAR. I'VE STILL GOT MALT. AND KEEP AN EYE OUT FOR BOTTLES...

THANKS, SID.

SURE.

YOU TAKE ANY MORE PICTURES?

I TOOK THE LAST ONE ON THE FILM ROLL.

I WANT TO SEE THEM.

DON'T HOLD YOUR BREATH. WE *CAN'T AFFORD* TO GET THEM DEVELOPED. IT'S FUN, BUT I DON'T KNOW WHY I BOTHERED.

YOU SHOULD MAKE YOURSELF SCARCE TODAY, SID.

'KAY.

BUT WHERE WILL WE GO?

— MARCELLE —
PHOTOGRAPHY STUDIO
— J. SHULMAN PROP. —

OPEN

DING DING

GOT A FILM.

NAME?

VENDITELLI.

HMM.

TWENTY-FIVE CENTS. COME BACK TUESDAY.

UH. NEED A DELIVERY BOY? ODD JOBS?

NO, SON. TRADE DOESN'T WORK THAT WAY.

OKAY. THANKS.

WAIT!

YOU GET A FREE FILM WHEN YOU BRING ONE IN FOR DEVELOPING.

I TOOK THE LONG WAY HOME.

NEED YOUR *FENCE* PAINTED, MA'AM?

ALL TAKEN CARE OF.

IT'S A *HOT DAY,* SIR. NEED YOUR *DOG* WALKED?

THEY DROVE ALL THE WAY TO *LAKE SIMCOE* AND THERE'S THIS SIGN...

...FRANNIE SWORE IT READ...

NO DOGS OR JEWS ALLOWED

I'DA *BUSTED* THEIR *FAT MOUTHS.*

AH, BUST 'EM IN THE RING. LIKE *SAMMY LUFTSPRING!*

OR *MAXIE BAER.* I LOVED IT WHEN HE BEAT *SCHMELING.* GOT IT OVER MY HEART.

HE'S GONNA BE FIRST HEAVYWEIGHT CHAMP FOR US!

YOU MIGHT NEED THEM HERE. LOOK AT THIS.

Members of the Swastika Club say it is their intention to prevent a foreign invasion fouling the beaches with their immigrant disregard for manners and private property.

"It's not that they're Jewish," one member claimed. "It's the way they behave, littering and walking half-naked. Why should every Rachel and Sammy think--

WELL, THE MAYOR SAID THAT HITLER STUFF--

FORGET ABOUT WHAT THE MAYOR *SAID*! YOU READ WHAT'S *HAPPENING* IN GERMANY?

IT'S GONNA HAPPEN *HERE* UNLESS WE STAND UP FOR OURSELVES. THAT'S WHY THE UNIONS HAD THAT *RALLY* BACK IN JULY.

LISTEN TO THE MAN! THEY *MARCH*, WE DO SOMETHING ABOUT IT.

OLD SAYING: GO SLOW, YOU'LL GET THERE FASTER.

SIDNEY! HOW'S YOUR *POP*?

OH, *GUS!* HE'S OKAY. I--

I KNOW YOU'RE GONNA ASK. I DON'T NEED ANY HELP. BUT *STICK AROUND* IF YOU WANT. YOU PUT SOME MEAT ON YOUR BONES AND I'LL TEACH YOU TO USE THAT PEP IN THE *RING.*

BY THE TIME I LEFT STARR'S, IT WAS A *SCORCHER.*

NEED ANY HELP?

NOT *TODAY.* BUT GRAB A COUPLE CHIPS FROM THE BACK AND *COOL* YOURSELF!

THANKS, MISTER.

LATER.

HOUSEHOLD CHORES. NEWSPAPERS WERE FOR MORE THAN READING.

TOILET TISSUE, FOR ONE.

RRRIP!

SAY...

POP AND TERESA WEREN'T HOME FROM WORK WHEN WE LEFT THAT EVENING.

SUNNYSIDE WAS THE *PLACE* TO BE ON A SUMMER NIGHT.

THERE WAS A COOL BREEZE OFF THE LAKE.

THE FERRIS WHEEL...

THE GAMES...

THE FLYER...

...AND THE RUMBLE OF FEET ON THE BOARDWALK.

OVER THERE!

AIN'T SHE SWEET? READY? TWO, THREE, FOUR...

AW, PLUG--

AAAAIN'T SHE SWEEEET...?

OH, AIN'T SHE NIIICE...?

I WAS LOUSY.

PLUG WAS GREAT.

WON'T YOU COME **HOME**, BILL BAI-**LEY**...

...WON'T YOU COME **HOME**...

SAW A **COP** CHASING A **CROOK**--

IT WAS **SO HOT** THEY WERE BOTH **WALKING**!

HA HA HA

SAY, **YOU'RE SMARTER** THAN **I LOOK**.

HA HA HA HA

THANK YOU! HERE'S ANOTHER!

PLUG! MOVE! COPPER!

ALL RIGHT, *BREAK IT UP!* NO *PANHANDLING!*

HEY, WE'RE NOT--

I SAID *BREAK IT UP!* MOVE *ALONG.*

THE COINS!

THEY'RE FALLING THROUGH THE *CRACKS!*

BETCHA I MADE MORE'N YOU.

ASK ME NO QUESTIONS AND I'LL TELL YOU NO *LIES*.

Y'KNOW, IT'S NOT SO BAD HERE. WE OUGHT TO MAKE THIS A REGULAR GRIFT.

IF YOU DID SO GREAT, IT WAS THANKS TO *US*.

SHARE UP.

THANKS TO *THESE*, BROTHER.

YOU WANT SOME *REAL DOUGH*, YOU AND PLUG COME WITH ME TOMORROW.

NOW I GOT PLACES TO GO. *SEE YA*, SUCKERS!

DON'T GO TOMORROW. HE'S HORRIBLE.

GUYS! I JUST SPOKE TO A TEACHER FROM HARBORD COLLEGIATE. RUNS THE GLEE CLUB!

HE LOVED US. TOLD ME TO BE SURE TO COME SEE HIM WHEN I GET THERE!

THAT'S WHERE WE'LL *ALL* BE GOING!

WELL, *YOU* WILL. IN SEPTEMBER. ME...

IF UNCLE TONY'S BUSINESS PICKS UP, MAYBE I'LL HAVE TO-- I MEAN, I *WANT* TO...

WE **ALL** WISH WE HAD JOBS.

YOU SHOULD BE **AMELIA EARHART**, ROSIE. FLY AROUND THE WORLD AND TAKE PICTURES.

AND YOU SHOULD BE **BING CROSBY**. A RADIO STAR, AND IN THE PICTURES!

WHAT ABOUT SID?

THE FIRST **JEWISH PRIME MINISTER!**

AW, YOU GUYS...

SO HOW MUCH DID WE MAKE?

NOT COUNTING WHAT FELL THROUGH THE CRACKS, NINETEEN CENTS.

I BET WE LOST ANOTHER TWENTY-FIVE UNDER THE BOARDWALK.

GEEZ! WELL, I KNOW WHAT I'M SPENDING MY SHARE ON: DINNER.

FRIES

SNACKS

DRINKS

FRENCH FRIES

ICE CREAM

CORN DOGS

SO NOW IT'S MY TURN FOR A PLAN.

LOOK WHAT WAS IN THE PAPER.

PROFESSOR **MERCER** AT THE UNIVERSITY BIOLOGY LAB ON COLLEGE STREET IS PAYING **A PENNY APIECE** FOR COCKROACHES. HERE'S THE ADDRESS AND EVERYTHING!

SID, YOU'RE A **GENIUS**!

KEEP THIS UP AND BEFORE YOU KNOW IT, WE'LL BE SINGING...

WE'RE IN THE **MONEYYY**... WE'RE IN THE **MONEYYY**...

MAYBE WE'D **HAVE** WHAT IT TOOK TO GET **ALONG**...

Chapter 3
Sucker Punch

CATCHING ROACHES ISN'T AS EASY AS YOU'D THINK...

...EVEN WHEN YOUR PLACE HAS PLENTY.

COCKROACHES LIKE THE DARK. STRIKE A LIGHT...

...AND THEY'RE GONE.

BUT I'D HAD ALL DAY TO THINK ABOUT IT.

GIVE ME THAT SHEET OF NEWSPAPER AND YOUR LARD CAN.

UGH, I CAN *HEAR* THEM.

GET THE *BUCKET READY*, PLUG. GOT THE *COVER*, ROSIE?

NOW!

GAH!

THEY'RE **ON** ME! THEY'RE **ON** ME!

GET THE--

--LID...**ON**...

DONE!

HUFF HUFF HUFF

YES?

WE BROUGHT COCKROACHES.

LOTS OF THEM!

AH.

I'M SORRY, KIDS. WE'VE ALREADY GOT ALL WE NEED.

IT DIDN'T SAY ANYTHING ABOUT A LIMIT!

I KNOW, BUT THE PROFESSOR SAYS WE HAVE ENOUGH.

C'MON, SID. LET'S GO.

NOT A CHANCE. YOU PAY US FOR THESE OR I'LL LET THE WHOLE BUCKET GO, *RIGHT HERE*!

SID!

NOW, JUST A MINUTE.

I'LL *DO IT*!

ALL RIGHT. WE'LL DUMP THE BUCKET INTO THIS EMPTY TERRARIUM, BUT WE'LL HAVE TO ESTIMATE HOW MANY. ARE THERE A LOT?

MUST BE A *COUPLE HUNDRED.* I SCOOPED THEM ON GREASED PAPER.

LET'S FIND OUT.

BUT, THERE WERE--

THIS COULD BE YOUR PROBLEM.

SIX **LOUSY** CENTS...

IT WAS A SWELL IDEA.

IDEAS DON'T **COUNT.**

THEY DO SOMETIMES.

67

I HEAR THERE WAS SOME DOINGS ON THE **BOARDWALK** LAST NIGHT. YOU WEREN'T **THERE** WERE YOU?

AT **SUNNYSIDE**?

UH-UH. EAST END. LATE. OUT IN BALMY BEACH.

NO. I WASN'T THERE.

GOOD. STAY OUT OF IT.

HA! YEP.

JUST LIKE YOUR POP.

YOU KNOW, YOUR POP COULDA BEEN A GOOD FIGHTER.

BUT HE WAS HOTHEADED. WOULDN'T LISTEN. HE'D GET ANGRY, SWING WILD.

YOU ALWAYS GOT TO THINK. YOU FORGET TO THINK, THAT'S WHEN YOU GET POPPED.

YOU HIT, EXPECT A HIT. YOU *GET HIT,* HIT BACK. SOUNDS SIMPLE, DON'T IT?

PATIENCE, SIDNEY. THINK. IT'S EASY TO FORGET.

DON'T FORGET.

HEY--

ME AND SOME OF THE BOYS AT HI'S HEARD THEY WAS GOING TO BE WEARING THEM ON THE BOARDWALK LAST NIGHT, PARADING AROUND.

SO WE TOOK A LITTLE TRIP ON DOWN AND SURE ENOUGH, THEY'RE WEARIN' 'EM.

KEEP OUR BEACHES CLEA[N]

SAY NO JEW

SWEATSHIRTS EVEN, WITH THAT CRAZY CROSS EMBROIDERED. THERE WAS GIRLS HAD THEM ON THEIR SWIMSUITS.

SO WE PASS BACK AND FORTH A COUPLE OF TIMES. THEY'RE GOIN' "HIYA, PAL," TO EACH OTHER.

THERE WAS COPS EVERYWHERE. THE BOYS WAS STEAMING TO MIX IT UP, BUT SCARED TO START SOMETHING. SAMMY AND MUTT BOTH HAVE MONEY FIGHTS COMING UP.

SO I WALK UP TO THIS LUG, BIGGEST ONE THERE, AND COOL AS A CUCUMBER I--

SO THEY DO.

THE BOYS ALL CHEERED AND RODE ME HOME ON THEIR SHOULDERS.

EVERYBODY'S TALKING ABOUT HOW IT WAS ALL ON ACCOUNT OF *ME*. LUCK O' THE IRISH.

WOW.

SO, LIKE I SAID, YOU, ME AND PLUG TONIGHT. THERE'S ANOTHER BALL GAME AT THE PITS.

WE'LL *TEACH 'EM* TO MESS WITH US. DON'T BE LATE.

Chapter 4

Devil's Deal

HEY, POP.

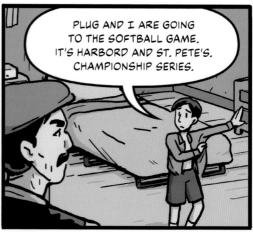

PLUG AND I ARE GOING TO THE SOFTBALL GAME. IT'S HARBORD AND ST. PETE'S. CHAMPIONSHIP SERIES.

IF IT'S HARBORD, OUR CROWD WILL BE THERE. BUT DON'T GET MIXED UP IN ANYTHING. THIS IS A BAD TIME.

I'LL BE CAREFUL.

AND DON'T BE *LATE*.

I-- I NEED TO TALK TO YOU ABOUT SOMETHING.

PLUG SAYS YOU'RE GOING TO THE GAME.

I'M **COMING TOO**! MARIA AND ANGIE WILL MEET US.

BUT--

ANGIE! MARIA!

LADIES...

HI THERE.

THERE WON'T BE TROUBLE, WILL THERE? BECAUSE HARBORD IS **JEWISH**?

I TOLD MY MAMA PLUG AND HIS FRIEND WOULD BE ESCORTING US.

WHY WOULD THERE BE TROUBLE?

HAVEN'T YOU SEEN THE PAPERS?

NO, WHAT'S GOING ON?

THERE WAS TROUBLE DOWN IN THE EAST END, BALMY BEACH.

CHRISTIE PITS ISN'T *EAST END*.

SOMETIMES PEOPLE DON'T LIKE ANYONE WHO ISN'T FROM THEIR NEIGHBOURHOOD.

JEEPERS, THIS IS *EXCITING*! I'M GLAD MAMA DOESN'T KNOW.

WILLOWVALE WAS A BIG PARK. HARBORD PLAYGROUND VS. ST. PETER'S CHURCH WAS ONLY ONE OF THE GAMES GOING ON.

HOW CAN WE HELP **TOMMY** WITH THE **GIRLS** WATCHING? IF THEY SEE WHAT WE'RE UP TO...

MAYBE WE WON'T SEE HIM AT ALL.

I BET HE'LL BE OVER WITH THE CROWD AT THE HARDBALL DIAMOND. LET'S GO TO THE SOFTBALL INSTEAD.

GIRLS, IT'S SO HOT **FIRE HYDRANTS** CHASE **DOGS**!

PLUG.

I BET YOU COULD TAKE SOME GREAT SNAPS HERE.

DON'T I **WISH**!

THE **GAME**, ALL THE PEOPLE...

THAT MAN LOOKS LIKE A MOBSTER.

SHE COULD BE A MOVIE STAR.

AND OVER THERE, HE'S A PICKPOCKET. AND THOSE TWO ARE IN LOVE...

HA, YEAH. SURE. LOVE.

SAY, GOSH, I KEEP FORGETTING...

I, UH, GOT A LITTLE SOMETHING--

OOF!

WELL, *HELLO* AGAIN. ROSIE YOUR *GAL*, SID? *LUCKY DOG!*

WHAT? GEEZ, TOMMY...

'SCUSE US, SISTER. WE GOT A COUPLE OF THINGS TO DO. WON'T TAKE LONG.

AW, TOMMY, I-- I CAN'T RIGHT NOW.

I TOLD YOU 'BOUT THIS *TWICE* AND YOU NEVER SAID BOO. YOU CAN'T BACK OUT NOW.

OR DO YOU WANTA LET *PLUG* DOWN, TOO?

WE'LL MEET YOU HERE IN TEN MINUTES. TOPS.

NEVER LET DAMES CALL THE SHOTS. THAT'S HOW MY UNCLE ENDED UP IN **KINGSTON PEN.**

I DON'T THINK WE SHOULD DO THIS, TOMMY.

WHAT, ARE YOU **RICH** ALL OF A SUDDEN? A **ROCKEFELLER**? WE'RE LIKE **ROBIN HOODS.** TAKE FROM THE RICH AND GIVE TO THE POOR. ALL FOR ONE AND ONE FOR ALL!

ALL FOR ONE IS THE THREE MUSKETEERS.

OKAY THEN, WE'RE **COWBOYS.**

I DON'T SEE A LOT OF RICH PEOPLE AROUND HERE.

THEY **HIDE** IT.

NOW, SPREAD OUT. PLUG STALLS, SID'S DUKE MAN, LIKE USUAL.

TEN MINUTES. WE CAN'T LEAVE THE GIRLS FOR LONG.

NOD NOD

NOT SO FAST.

POLICE. YOU'RE COMING DOWN TO THE STATION.

DON'T TRY IT. YOU'RE IN ENOUGH TROUBLE ALREADY.

LET'S GO.

EMPTY YOUR POCKETS.

LOOKIT! HE'S THE ONE YOU WANT! YOU STINKIN' THIEF, GETTING ME AND PLUG IN YOUR JAM!

WHA-- HEY!

I NEVER **SEEN** IT BEFORE! HE MUSTA **STUCK IT** THERE!

THERE'S A RENT RECEIPT FOR THOMAS MORGAN.

NO **KIDDIN'**. I KNOW HIM, HE'S THE UMPIRE AT THE **BALL GAME**! THE LITTLE YID STOLE THE UMPIRE'S WALLET?

WHO YOU CALLING **YID**? NAME'S **RYAN**!

SHUT UP, **LEPOFSKY**. WE KNOW ALL ABOUT YOU. YOU'RE A MECHANIC, JUST LIKE YOUR UNCLE.

AND WE KNOW ABOUT **YOU TWO** AS WELL.

I'M IN THE **RED SQUAD**. WE TELL LUXE GARMENT THEIR WORKERS ARE RAISING **THIEVES**, YOUR PARENTS WILL LOSE THEIR JOBS.

ESPECIALLY WHEN THEY TOOK PART IN THAT JULY STRIKE.

BUT YOU WON'T CARE. YOU'LL BE IN **REFORMATORY**. AND LEPOFSKY WILL BE WITH HIS UNCLE, IN **KINGSTON PEN**.

PLEASE, MISTER. MY MAMMA NEEDS THAT JOB. MY PAPA HAS HIS **GAMBA FERITA**, AND MY NONNO--

WE SPEAK **ENGLISH** HERE.

A WOUNDED LEG. OUR FATHERS FOUGHT IN THE **WAR**...SIR.

THEY SHOULD HAVE BEEN GRATEFUL WE LET THEM SERVE THE EMPIRE. INSTEAD, THEY'RE **REDS** AND **UNION AGITATORS**. AND THEY RAISE **SCUM** LIKE YOU.

WHAT?

WE AIN'T NO *REDS*. WE'RE JUST *POOR KIDS.*

WE DON'T KNOW ABOUT UNION AGITATORS!

DON'T PLAY *STUPID.* ANARCHISTS, AGITATORS, COMMUNISTS: ALL IMMIGRANTS AND JEWS.

TIM BUCK'S NOT JEWISH!

SO, YOU KNOW THE HEAD OF THE CANADIAN COMMUNIST PARTY.

EVERYBODY KNOWS WHO HE IS. HE'S IN KINGSTON PEN. TOMMY'S RIGHT, MISTER. WE'RE JUST...POOR.

SHUT UP. YOU'RE ALSO GUILTY AS HELL.

BUT IF YOU *REALLY* WANT TO ACT LIKE BRITISH SUBJECTS...

...WE'LL GIVE YOU A CHANCE TO SHOW IT.

HOW? YOU NAME IT!

WHO'S THAT?

NEVER MIND. ALL YOU NEED TO KNOW IS HE'LL BE AT THE BALL GAME WEDNESDAY NIGHT. EVEN REDS LIKE A BALL GAME.

HE'LL HAVE A *PAPER* ON HIM, SOMEWHERE. WE WANT IT.

DONE.

MORE THAN THAT.

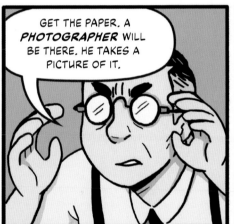

GET THE PAPER. A *PHOTOGRAPHER* WILL BE THERE. HE TAKES A PICTURE OF IT.

THEN YOU PUT IT BACK, SO OUR MAN NEVER KNOWS IT WAS GONE.

PUT IT *BA--*? BUT--

PIECE OF CAKE. WE DO THIS AND YOU MAKE OUR PROBLEM GO AWAY?

PROBLEMS LIKE YOU *NEVER* GO AWAY, LEPOFSKY. BUT THIS ONE COULD.

COULD OR WOULD?

C'MON, LEPOFSKY. YOU REALLY THINK YOU HAVE A *CHOICE*?

NOBODY GETS IN TROUBLE?

NOBODY FINDS OUT?

NOBODY LOSES THEIR JOB?

THAT'S THE DEAL?

DONE. WE'LL NEED THE PHOTO.

NO, YOU WON'T. AND YOU CAN PUT BACK THE MONEY AND POCKET KNIFE, TOO.

SOME JUST DON'T LEARN.

IT WAS JUST A GAG! CAN'T YOU TAKE A JOKE?

SHUT UP, LEPOFSKY.

WHY WE LET FOREIGNERS IN...

NAME'S *RYAN!*

AW, CORK IT, TOMMY.

YOU TRIED TO BLAME IT ALL ON *ME*!

'COURSE I DID, IT WAS ALL YOUR *FAULT*! YOU SHOULD'VE DITCHED THE TAKE ON THE WAY TO THE STATION. ANY FOOL KNOWS THAT!

GEE, *SORRY.* I'VE NEVER BEEN *ARRESTED* BEFORE.

GUYS! STOP *FIGHTING!*

WHAT MATTERS IS THAT WE'RE HERE NOW...

BYE BYE, *BLACKBIRD...*

...BYE BYEEEEE...

HOW DO WE DO IT?

SAME AS ALWAYS. ONLY DIFFERENCE IS, *SID'S* GONNA HAVE TO PUT IT BACK.

ME?

YEAH, HE'LL HAVE SEEN ME AND PLUG.

DON'T WORRY, I'LL SHOW YA TOMORROW. WE'LL PRACTISE.

DON'T WORRY? I WORRIED. IT'S HARD NOT TO IN A CELL.

THE SMELL WAS EVEN WORSE THAN THE MUSIC.

BYE...BYE...

I SAID *SHADDUP!*

FINALLY.

CLICK

ALL RIGHT, OUT!

LEPOFSKY, YOUR SISTER HAS PROMISED ME YOU WON'T RUN. BECAUSE *IF YOU DO*, WE'RE GOING TO SHUT HER DOWN.

AND IF WE SHUT *HER* DOWN, HER FRIEND *HARRY SUITCASE* IS GOING TO BE ANGRY WITH YOU. YOU DON'T WANT THAT, DO YOU?

N-- NO!

HM. MAYBE JAIL MAKES YOU SMARTER.

CHRISTIE PITS. WEDNESDAY NIGHT. SEVEN O'CLOCK.

WE'RE WATCHING YOU. BREATHE A WORD ABOUT THIS AND YOUR *PARENTS* ARE ON THE STREET.

AND YOU'RE IN JAIL.

...AND WE GOT THE **SERGEANT** TO CARRY THE **MACHINE GUN**!

THAT MUD WAS SO THICK--

HAHA!

SID!

FEDERICO!

SEE? I TOLD YOU IT WOULD WORK OUT.

JUST A LITTLE MISUNDERSTANDING. THEY'RE FREE TO GO. THERE WAS SOME TROUBLE AT THE PARK.

WE HEARD.

HARRY!

LET'S GO.

NOW, KEEP YOUR NOSES **CLEAN**, BOYS! OFF YOU GO.

GOOD TO **SEE YOU**, BERT! BEST TO THE MISSUS.

OLD TIMES!

DON'T BE A **STRANGER**!

IT'S STILL HOT. WHAT TIME IS IT?

AFTER MIDNIGHT.

WH-- WHO WERE YOU TALKING TO?

BERT ALLISON. WE WERE IN THE ARMY TOGETHER.

DIDN'T I *TELL* YOU TO--

ROSIE TOLD US THEY GRABBED YOU AT THE PARK.

DID THEY *HURT* YOU?

N-- NO!

TRUST THE POLICE TO THINK THAT **WE** STARTED IT.

BUT... STARTED...?

WHAT DID ROSIE SAY?

YOU DIDN'T EVEN **SEE**? AND THEY GRABBED YOU ANYWAY. SCUM.

UM, YEAH...I GUESS THEY GOT US RIGHT AT THE START...

JUST BECAUSE OF THE WAY YOU LOOKED. AND ALL THE TIME IT WAS THAT PIT GANG.

BERT SAID THEY STARTED FLASHING A BANNER--A **SWASTIKA**--YELLING **JEWS OUT OF THE PARK**.

THERE WERE SOME TANGLES, BUT OF COURSE IT WAS MOSTLY **US** THE COPS PUSHED AROUND.

OH, UM, *RIGHT!* WE DIDN'T EVEN *KNOW!*

SINCE WHEN DID THAT MATTER?

LISTEN, SID: YOU HAVE THE RIGHT TO GO ANYWHERE, DO ANYTHING, BE ANYTHING. THAT'S *SUPPOSED* TO BE WHY WE FOUGHT A WAR.

MAYBE THERE'LL BE ANOTHER WAR BEFORE WE REALLY CAN. BUT OUR DAY *WILL COME*, EVEN WITH THIS HITLER IN GERMANY.

BUT RIGHT NOW, THIS IS A TIME TO KEEP YOUR NOSE CLEAN. THERE ARE THINGS, *IMPORTANT* THINGS THAT-- THAT--

NEVER MIND. JUST REMEMBER: WE'RE LUCKY TO HAVE FRIENDS LIKE THE VENDITELLIS. WE HELP EACH OTHER, NO MATTER WHAT.

GOT IT?

SURE, POP.

NO MATTER WHAT.

LOOK!

LET'S GO. IT'S LATE.

WHO WON THE GAME?

WE DID. HARBORD. CLUTCH SINGLE IN THE TENTH.

FINAL GAME IS WEDNESDAY NIGHT.

Chapter 5

Tough Spot to Pick

POP WAS GONE WHEN I WOKE THE NEXT MORNING.

I WAS STILL IN BIG TROUBLE.

ROSIE COVERING FOR ME AND PLUG AT HOME WASN'T GOING TO SQUARE THINGS WITH THE COPS.

AND HOW WAS I EVER GOING TO PUT BACK SOMETHING TOMMY STOLE FROM A MARK?

WHAT WOULD HAPPEN IF I GOT CAUGHT? THIS WASN'T SOME ADVENTURE STORY.

Sid, we need:
eggs
bread
milk
canned tomatoes
potatoes
carrots

money on table

I HALF-HOPED TOMMY WOULD TAKE OFF, IN SPITE OF WHOEVER HARRY SUITCASE WAS.

THEN I REMEMBERED WHAT THAT WOULD MEAN FOR PLUG AND ME.

IT DIDN'T MATTER THAT THERE WASN'T MUCH TO EAT. I DIDN'T FEEL LIKE IT ANYWAY.

CIAO, NONNO. WHERE ARE FREDO AND ROSA?

FREDO HELPS HIS PAPA. ROSA GOES TO MARKET. HAVE YOU EATEN?

YES, THANKS.

I WASN'T SURE WHERE ANGELO WAS, SO I KIDDED, IN CASE HE HEARD ME.

THOSE DON'T LOOK VERY CLEAN TO ME.

117

IT WAS ANOTHER SCORCHER OF A DAY, BRIGHT AND SUNNY.

BUT EVERYWHERE I WENT...

...I FELT A SHADOW.

LISTEN, I... WELL...THANK--

DON'T THANK ME. *TELL* ME.

WHAT WAS *GOING ON* LAST NIGHT, SID? PLUG WOULDN'T SAY ANYTHING.

NOTHING! IT WAS ALL A-- A *MIX-UP*. THEY LET US GO. IT WAS OTHER TROUBLE IN THE PARK.

DON'T LIE!

IT'S *TRUE*! ASK YOUR *PAPA*, ASK *MY POP*!

AND AFTER, WE SAW SOMEONE PAINTING--

I ALREADY HEARD. THE WHOLE NEIGHBOURHOOD HAS BEEN TALKING ABOUT IT.

WELL THEN?

THAT ALL CAME *LATER*. I WATCHED YOU THREE LAST NIGHT. TOMMY HAD YOU UP TO SOMETHING.

WERE YOU THIEVING WITH HIM?

NO!

DON'T *LIE*! I LIED FOR YOU LAST NIGHT. I *WON'T* DO IT AGAIN.

UH...

IT'S JUST THAT, UH...

BE *HONEST* WITH ME, SID. WHAT ARE YOU DOING? IF PLUG GETS IN TROUBLE...

I TOLD HER.

YOU *ARE* STEALING!

HOW ELSE CAN WE GET MONEY? THERE'S NO WORK. WE ONLY TAKE FROM--

DON'T GIVE ME THAT **ROBIN HOOD** MALARKEY!

OKAY! ANYWAY, THEY CAUGHT US. WE WON'T DO IT ANYMORE.

AND THERE'S A WAY FOR US TO SQUARE IT WITH THE POLICE. TOMORROW. AT THE GAME.

WHAT DO YOU HAVE TO DO?

NOTHING. NEVER MIND. TAKE SOMETHING AND PUT IT BACK.

TAKE WHAT? FROM WHO?

THIS THING. NOT MONEY, A PAPER. FROM THIS GUY.

WHO IS HE?

I DON'T KNOW. A RED AGITATOR OR SOMETHING.

HE HAS A PAPER, WE TAKE IT. THEY SNAP A PHOTO, WE PUT IT BACK. NO HARM DONE. NOT EVEN **STEALING!**

THAT SOUNDS FISHY...

NEVER MIND. WE DO IT, THAT'S ALL.

LISTEN, ROSIE, THIS IS FOR YOU. I WAS GOING TO GIVE IT TO YOU LAST NIGHT, BEFORE WE--

A *FILM*? WHAT'S ALL THIS, SID?

I, UH, TOOK YOUR SNAPS IN FOR DEVELOPING. FOR A SURPRISE, LIKE. THEY SHOULD BE READY TODAY.

AND YOU GET THE FILM FREE.

OH MY *GOSH*! THANKS!

BUT WHERE DID YOU GET THE MONEY TO...?

...OH.

I CAN'T TAKE THIS, SID.

WHAT? **NO!**

COME **ON**, ROSIE! IT'S ALREADY PAID.

BUT NOW IT'S LIKE I STOLE IT TOO.

AND WHAT YOU'RE DOING FOR THE POLICE. IT **CAN'T** BE RIGHT. I DON'T TRUST THEM.

BUT, ROSIE, WE **HAVE** TO!

YOU DIDN'T HAVE TO STEAL IN THE **FIRST PLACE**. THIS IS JUST STEALING AGAIN.

WE'LL GO TO *JAIL* IF WE DON'T!

IT CAN'T BE *RIGHT*!

IS IT RIGHT FOR YOUR PAPA TO BOOTLEG HIS *MOONSHINE*? IS *THAT* ALL RIGHT?

PAPA'S CRIPPLED! HE CAN'T--

OH, I *DON'T KNOW*! WHY DID YOU HAVE TO BRING *THAT* UP?

ROSIE, WAIT! I'M...SORRY...

I'M SUCH A *SHMUCK*!

STARK

IF IT COMES TO A ROUGHHOUSE, A LEAD PIPE WORKS THE BEST...

CRASH!

SIDNEY, MY LITTLE RAY OF SUNSHINE!

HAPPY AS THE DAY IS LONG, OR IN AN UNFAIR FIGHT?

UH. YOU SAID IT. SORRY ABOUT THE--

WE'LL FILL IT OVER HERE.

SEE THAT PALOOKA OVER THERE?

EVERY SO OFTEN HE HITS BELOW THE BELT.

WHAT FOR? HE'S *HUGE*.

DOESN'T MATTER.

I DUNNO IF HE DOES IT 'CAUSE HE CAN, OR IF HE JUST CAN'T HELP HIMSELF.

SOMEBODY HITTING *YOU* BELOW THE BELT?

MORE LIKE I DON'T EVEN KNOW WHAT *THE RULES* ARE...

WHAT'D I TELL YOU LAST TIME?

YOU HIT, EXPECT A HIT. YOU GET HIT, HIT BACK.

WHAT ELSE?

OW!

WHAP

YOU'RE *HIT.* WHADDA YOU DO NOW?

GEEZ! HIT BACK.

BEFORE THAT.

ACK!

WHUP!

HEY!

WHADDA YOU DO FIRST? TELL ME!

I DUNNO...

YOU THINK, SIDNEY. *THINK!*

THAT'S WHAT I'M TRYING TO DO!

NO, YOU'RE NOT. LOOK AT YOU, KEYED UP TO SHOOT FIRST. YOU'RE GETTING A KICK OUTTA BEING ANGRY.

YOU PICK YOUR SPOT. RIGHT, CARL?

YOU SAID IT.

SOMETIMES IT'S WORTH TAKING A PUNCH OR TWO.

THEN: *POW!*

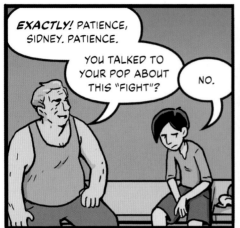

EXACTLY! PATIENCE, SIDNEY. PATIENCE.

YOU TALKED TO YOUR POP ABOUT THIS "FIGHT"?

NO.

MAYBE YOU SHOULD.

WORD IS, HE'S A THINKER THESE DAYS.

I DID THE ERRANDS, THEN TRIED TO LIE LOW, WONDERING IF TOMMY WOULD COME BY.

HOW WOULD YOU PUT SOMETHING BACK IN A POCKET? AND WHICH POCKET?

GAH!

GEVALT!

LET'S JUST SAY I WASN'T A NATURAL...

131

MY BLUE HEAVEN...

LET'S COOL OFF. I'VE GOT ENOUGH FOR A SODA EACH.

SWELL. SHOULD I GET ROSIE?

DOES SHE WANT TO TALK TO US RIGHT NOW?

PROB'LY NOT.

WHAT ARE WE GONNA *DO*, PLUG?

I DON'T THINK WE'VE GOT A **CHOICE.** MAMMA'S AND YOUR POP'S JOBS, REFORMATORY...

BUT I'M NOT SLICK ENOUGH PUT SOMETHING *BACK*.

YOU'LL HAVE TO BE.

WHAT IF IT'S AN INSIDE POCKET?

LOOK, LET'S TRY IT. TAKE THIS--

UH-OH. SPEAK OF THE DEVIL.

I HEARD WHY HARRY SUITCASE IS CALLED THAT: HE PUT A GUY IN ONE.

THAT'S *CRAZY*! *YOU CAN'T* FIT SOMEONE IN A *SUITCASE* UNLESS YOU...

...OH.

HOW'S *TRICKS*, BOYS?

SID DOESN'T THINK HE CAN PUT IT BACK.

AWW!

THAT'S WHY *WE'RE* HERE. GIMME THAT PAPER, PLUG. WE'RE GONNA *PRACTISE*.

IT'S SAME AS USUAL TILL THE END: PLUG STALLS, I LIFT, SID'S DUKE.

RIP!

SINCE HE AIN'T BEEN *SEEN*, HE'S THE ONE PUTS IT BACK.

IT'S ALL ABOUT *MISDIRECTION*, LIKE WHEN PLUG BUMPS THE MARK.

AND YOU NEED A LITTLE *CAN-DO* OUTLOOK. *C'MON!*

WHAT'S IN YER *POCKETS*, BOYS?

BUT I CAN'T *BUMP* THE GUY! PLUG WILL ALREADY HAVE DONE THAT. HE'LL *SUSPECT!*

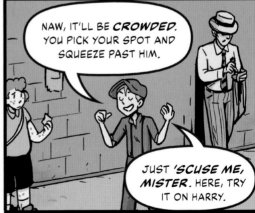

NAW, IT'LL BE *CROWDED*. YOU PICK YOUR SPOT AND SQUEEZE PAST HIM.

JUST *'SCUSE ME, MISTER*. HERE, TRY IT ON HARRY.

TRY IT ON SOMEONE ELSE.

TRY IT ON *ME*.

THERE! PUSH UP AGAINST PLUG FROM BEHIND, SAY "'SCUSE ME," AND MOVE THE PAPER.

SORRY!

DIDN'T FEEL A THING!

BECAUSE I NEVER GOT IT *IN* YOUR POCKET.

TRY IT AGAIN.

SORRY!

ERK!

ACK.

ENOUGH.

THIS GUY YOU HAFTA SQUEEZE, HE A RED? A COMMIE?

I GUESS. SOME KIND OF AGITATOR.

I *HATE* REDS. THEY GET THE COPS WORKED UP. THEN THE COPS PAY TOO MUCH ATTENTION TO *EVERYBODY.*

LOOK, KID. YOU CAN'T PASS THE PAPER, JUST RUN UP TO HIM WITH IT AND SAY HE DROPPED IT. IF YER LUCKY, HE'LL GIVE YOU A *NICKEL.*

BUT THEN HE'LL SEE ME. AND KNOW THE PAPER WAS GONE.

SURE, HE CAN MAKE YOU, BUT HE WON'T PUT TWO AND TWO TOGETHER.

NOW WE'RE GETTING OUTTA HERE. IT'S *STINKING HOT* AND I'M UP WAY TOO EARLY.

IT'S AFTERNOON!

WHAT'S *THAT* GOT TO DO WITH IT?

FEEL BETTER? ME NEITHER.

I STILL WANT A SODA, THOUGH.

POP BROUGHT SAUSAGE HOME THAT NIGHT. ROSIE COOKED IT, AND WE ATE WITH THE VENDITELLIS.

FOR THE FIRST FEW MINUTES, IT WAS CHEWING INSTEAD OF TALKING. ROSIE WOULDN'T LOOK MY WAY.

...*DIO HOUR*, BROUGHT TO YOU BY THE MAKERS OF *SIGNET SOAP*...

I WISH *WE* HAD A RADIO.

THAT'S WHAT *NEIGHBOURS* ARE FOR.

BUT THEN WE COULD GET *AMOS 'N' ANDY*.

I'SE REGUSTED!

HA HAHA HA HA HA HA HA HA HA HA HA HA HA HA

THAT WAS GOOD!

I WAS SURPRISED WHEN AMOS 'N' ANDY CAME TO TORONTO. THEY SOUND COLOURED AND THEY'RE **WHITE**!

EVERYONE KNOWS THAT, MAMMA.

MY CUSTOMERS NEVER TALKED THAT WAY. REMEMBER THE BRAITHWAITES?

AND THE **CARTERS**! WE SEE GEORGE AT SCHOOL.

CARL AT THE GYM HAS AN ACCENT, BUT NOT LIKE **THAT**.

MAYBE IT'S JUST AMERICANS.

ANGELO AND I MET COLOURED SOLDIERS IN FRANCE.

DID THEY TALK LIKE THAT?

NO. THE SOLDIERS DIDN'T MANGLE THE WORDS LIKE AMOS AND ANDY DO ON THE RADIO.

SOME HAD ACCENTS, BUT EVERYONE DID. *WE* HAD ACCENTS, TO EVERYONE ELSE.

IT WOULD BE SWELL TO HEAR DIFFERENT ACCENTS AROUND *HERE*.

HA! THE GOVERNMENT HASN'T LET IN CHINESE SINCE 1923. NOW THEY FEEL THE SAME ABOUT US.

MAKES YOU WONDER HOW *ANY OF US* GOT IN. I GUESS THEY NEED SOMEONE TO SWEAT FOR THEM.

OLD SAYING: IF THE RICH COULD HIRE PEOPLE TO *DIE FOR THEM*, THE POOR WOULD MAKE A *NICE LIVING*.

WE MAKE LESS THAN WE DID IN *'29*.

BUT THAT'S *THE DEPRESSION*. SOME DEAL SQUARE; THEY'RE NOT ALL *ORANGEMEN*. LOOK AT BERT LAST NIGHT, AND HIM A COPPER AND ALL.

IT'S **MORE** THAN THE **DEPRESSION**. BUT YOU'RE RIGHT, BERT'S A **MENSCH**. TOO BAD THERE AREN'T MORE OF HIM.

INSTEAD WE GET THAT DAMN **PIT GANG** AND THOSE **SWASTIKA CLUBS**.

THE MAYOR SAYS HE'S GOING TO **BAN THE SWASTIKA**. IT WAS IN THE PAPERS--

BELCH!

HO-LEE **MACK'REL!**

HA HA HA HA HA H

IN SPITE OF EVERYTHING, WE WERE HAPPY FOR A MOMENT. LIKE FAMILY. AND IT WAS MORE THAN JUST THE HALF-FORGOTTEN FEELING OF BEING FULL.

BUT ROSIE STILL WOULDN'T LOOK ME IN THE EYE.

AFTER DINNER, I THOUGHT ABOUT TELLING POP.

POP, I--

I'M BEAT. BUT I HAVE TO GO OUT.

WHERE?

I PROMISED FRIENDS. *PINOCHLE.* I WON'T BE LATE. HOW'S YOUR READING?

FINE.

YOU REMEMBER WHAT I SAID *LAST NIGHT*? ABOUT STICKING WITH OUR FRIENDS?

SURE.

WELL, IF SOMETIME I GOT IN A *JAM*, OR COULDN'T COME BACK--

FROM *PINOCHLE?*

NO. JUST SAYING. LOOK WHAT HAPPENED TO *YOU.*

THINGS ARE GETTING *WORSE.* REMEMBER THAT *STRIKE* LAST MONTH?

I REMEMBERED. BACK IN JULY, ALL THE GARMENT WORKERS HAD WALKED OFF THE JOB ONE AFTERNOON FOR A BIG ANTI-HITLER RALLY.

WELL, I HELPED ORGANIZE IT.

POLICE *REMEMBER* THINGS LIKE THAT. AND THEY'D JUST AS SOON BLAME *US* AS THOSE SWASTIKA THUGS.

THEY DON'T LIKE PEOPLE WHO *ORGANIZE* THINGS. UNLESS IT'S A *PINOCHLE GAME.*

I WON'T BE LATE.

THIS TIME I FOLLOWED SOONER.

THEN I GOT THE FEELING I'D HAD IN THE MORNING.

I TOOK A DETOUR...

...THEN ANOTHER.

AND DID SOME SIGHTSEEING...

BY THE TIME I GOT TO HI'S BILLIARDS, I HOPED I AND ANYONE TAILING ME WAS A LONG WAY FROM POP.

THINK THERE'LL BE *TROUBLE* IF HARBORD WINS?

LITTLE ITCH CUT SOME TWO BY FOURS, JUST IN CASE.

HEY, *KID*, WHERE'S THAT *TOMMY*? HE OWES ME A DOLLAR.

I DON'T KNOW.

HE HASN'T *SKIPPED*, HAS HE? I AIN'T SEEN HIM SINCE BEFORE THAT LITTLE SET-TO AT *BALMY BEACH.*

YOU WERE THERE WHEN TOMMY TORE OFF THE *SWASTIKA?*

TORE OFF--? GET YOUR HEAD READ, KID. *AL KAUFMAN* TORE OFF THE PATCH. TOMMY WASN'T EVEN *AT* BALMY BEACH.

WHAT KIND OF LINE WAS HE *FEEDING* YOU?

HE-- UM...

Chapter
6
Suicide Squeeze

WEDNESDAYS WERE NEVER MY FAVOURITE.

THIS ONE ESPECIALLY.

GOT SIX MONTHS IN JAIL, MY BACK TURNED TO THE WALL *FANNIN' THAT THING* WAS THE CAUSE OF IT ALL...

YOU GOT TO *FAN IT*...

WHAT'S THAT SONG?

A HILLBILLY TUNE. IT'S A PEACH. A FELLA OVER ON EUCLID WAS PLAYING IT ON A VICTROLA.

I HATE THE WORDS.

SPEAKING OF WORDS, YOU READ *A KICK IN THE KEISTER* BY *BEN DOVER?*

LET'S GO TO THE PARK NOW.

BUT IT'S ONLY ABOUT *FIVE O'CLOCK.*

I KNOW, PLUG, BUT THE WAITING IS *KILLING ME.* I HAFTA DO SOMETHING.

152

OKAY, BUT I NEED SOMETHING TO EAT FIRST. I'M *STARVING*.

WANT A *SUGAR SANDWICH*?

NO, THANKS. WHERE'S ROSIE?

I THINK SHE WENT TO THE MARKET.

SHE STILL *MAD*? SHE SURE WASN'T TALKING THIS MORNING.

WOMEN...

WHAT ARE YOU BRINGING YOUR UKE FOR?

WHO KNOWS? THERE'LL BE A CROWD. MAYBE I CAN *MAKE* A LITTLE SOMETHING.

OR IT COULD BE A GOOD *STALL.* YOU KNOW--

MAAARGIE, I'M ALWAYS THINKING OF *YOUUU...*

NOT BAD, HUH?

JEEPERS! IF YOU COULD DISTRACT THE GUY LIKE THAT WHEN I HAVE TO...

MAYBE I *CAN.* TOMMY'S SO GOOD HE PROB'LY DOESN'T NEED A STALL.

GOSH, I WISH.

ANYWAY, THIS EARLY WE CAN GET THE LAY OF THE LAND.

AS LONG AS WE DON'T GET CAUGHT BY THE *PIT GANG.*

HEY, YOU EVER READ *THE CROWDED OUTHOUSE* BY *PHIL TOBURSTIN?*

GEEZ, PLUG. AREN'T YOU EVEN *NERVOUS*?

I'M SO SCARED I CAN *TASTE IT.*

THIS IS THE ONLY WAY I CAN HANDLE IT.

I JUST WANT TO MAKE PEOPLE LAUGH.

I'M LAUGHING SO HARD I'M CRYING, BROTHER.

THIS IS CRAZY, SID! WHAT HAVE WE GOTTEN OURSELVES INTO?

NOW YOU ASK?

WHERE ARE THE COPS? THIS PLACE COULD **EXPLODE**!

PROBABLY GOT THEIR FEET UP AT THE STATION, HOPING WE GET THE STUFFING KNOCKED OUT OF US...

PLAY BALL!

GAME'S ON. WE BETTER GET DOWN THERE.

LOOKIT THE CROWD! HOW ARE WE GONNA *FIND* THE GUY?

I DUNNO. WE GOTTA TRY.

HONK!

HEY, **WATCH** IT!

WHAT ARE WE GONNA DO, SID? WE CAN'T GO BACK THERE.

WE *HAVE* TO.

OR IT WILL BE EVEN WORSE.

C'MON. KEEP YOUR EYES OPEN.

THAT'S *HIM*! THAT'S *THE MARK*!

HOW MANY *POCKETS* HAS HE GOT?

WHO KNOWS?

AND THERE'S THE *PHOTO GUY.*

WHERE'S TOMMY?

IF HE DOESN'T SHOW, WE'LL HAVE TO DO IT WITHOUT HIM.

I CAN'T PICK THE GUY'S POCKET! WHICH ONE IS THE PAPER EVEN *IN*?

WHAT IF I RAN SMACK INTO HIM?

WHAT IF YOU *DID*? HOW WILL I FIND IT? HOW WILL I PUT IT *BACK*?

SAME AS YOU WERE GOING TO.

"HEY, MISTER, YOU MUSTA DROPPED--"

WAIT... THERE HE IS!

HARRY PROBABLY HAD EYES ON TOMMY ALL OVER THE PARK.

PLUS OURS AND THE COPS'. HE WAS THE STAR.

ONLY TIME I'VE EVER BEEN *GLAD* TO SEE HIM.

PLAY YOUR *UKE*; GET HIS ATTENTION.

TAKE ME OUT TO THE *BALL GAAAAME...*

YOU READY?

AS I'LL NEVER BE.

WE BETTER SPLIT UP NOW...

I WAITED TO SEE WHICH ANGLE TOMMY WOULD TAKE THE MARK FROM.

BUT THERE WASN'T ONE. THE CROWD WAS PACKED TOO TIGHT.

IT WAS THE NINTH INNING. WHAT IF WE LOST HIM IN THE CRUSH WHEN EVERYONE LEFT? AROUND ME...

IKEY! KIKEY!

STEE-RIKE TWO! BOO!

STANDING IN THAT PARK MADE ME FEEL TINY AND ALONE.

ST. PETE'S FOREVER!

BAD CALL! PUT YOUR EYES BACK IN!

THE PLACE HAD GONE CUCKOO.

SWING AN' A MISS!

STRIKE HIM OUT! KILL THE BUM!

C'MON, HARBORD!

THEN...

HE'S MOVING!

...IT WAS TIME.

PRESS

WHOA THERE!

GEE, SORRY!

ARE YOU OKAY, SONNY?

WHAT THE--

FWEEET! FWEET!

SORRY!

YAY!

ST. PETE'S!

WE HAD TO WORK FAST BEFORE I LOST SIGHT OF THE MARK.

IKEY! KIKEY!

BOO! BOO!

HAR-BORD! HAR-BORD!

HARBORD, GO HOME!

HURRY!

PRES

HIT

171

HEY, SAMMY!

I BEEN WAITING FOR THIS, SAMMY.

S--STINKING *NAZI!*

CRASH!

CRACK!

WHUMP!

C'MON! WHERE'S PLUG?

WE NEED TO *MOVE!*

WANTA *TRY?*

YOU EVER *READ* THOSE PAPERS YOU SELL?

UHNNNNN...

WE SPEAK *ENGLISH* HERE.

IKEY! KIKEY!

I'LL *DO IT!*

STRIKE HIM OUT! KILL THE BUM!

CRASH!

HUFF...
HUFF...

THE FILM, ROSIE! SPOIL THE *FILM*!

SPOIL THE...?

THE FILM! *THE FILM!*

LET'S FIND PLUG AND GET OUT OF HERE.

NOD

YOU. THE PAPER. WHERE'S THE *PAPER*?

BUT YOU GOT A PIC--

THE CAMERA WAS *WRECKED*. WHERE'S *THE PAPER*? WHAT DID YOU DO WITH IT?

I-- I DROPPED IT. THIS GUY CAME AT US. MAYBE *HE'S* THE ONE WRECKED THE CAMERA?

SHUT UP.

GET OVER HERE!

AHHH! MY SHOULDER...

DA--! HOW BIG WAS IT?

LIKE *THIS*, MAYBE? I TOLD YOU, I DROPPED IT BACK--

QUICK! OVER THERE. *PAPER* ON THE GROUND, A *LIST*!

BUT--

COME ON!

GET OUT OF HERE!

LET'S GO!

LOOK!

C'MON, BOYS! LET'S *GET 'EM*!

GEVALT... I BEEN *WAITING* FOR THIS...

IS THAT SAMMY LUFTSPRING? SOMEBODY MUST HAVE PUT OUT THE *WORD*.

WHY DIDN'T SOMEBODY CALL THE *POLICE*?

MAYBE SOMEONE DID. THEY'RE NOT GOING TO HELP THE *LIKES* OF US.

YOU EVER GET YOUR DOLLAR?

I'M COLLECTIN' MORE THAN *THAT* TONIGHT!

LOOK, MORE *REINFORCEMENTS*! WE MIGHT NOT *NEED* ANY HELP!

SCREEEE

DON'T KID YOURSELF. IT LOOKED LIKE THAT MAN BACK THERE HELPED YOU. WHO *WAS* HE?

BERT ALLISON. HE-- HE'S A COP.

POLICE?

HE'S A **FRIEND.** KNEW PAPA AND MISTER K. FROM THE WAR.

OH... OH, **WAIT.**

I-- I HAVE TO--

NO, SID. WE HAVE TO **LEAVE.**

LET'S GET OUT OF HERE.

A GUY JUMPED ME. ROSIE HIT HIM WITH A CAMERA.

YOU *DID*?

THE ONLY THING *I* DON'T UNDERSTAND IS WHY YOU WANTED TO SPOIL THE FILM.

I THOUGHT THE COP WAS SUPPOSED TO TAKE THE PICTURE. WHY DID YOU SMASH THE CAMERA?

DID HE SNAP THE PAPER, SID? ARE WE OFF THE HOOK?

YEAH, BUT--

I-- I HAVE TO TALK TO POP.

POP! *POP!*

SID!

SID! WHERE YOU *BEEN?* WHAT'S GOING ON UP THERE? WE'RE HEARING ALL THESE WILD STORIES...

THEY'RE FIGHTING UP IN CHRISTIE PITS. THERE WAS A *SWASTIKA.*

BASTARDS!

ROSIE, FEDERICO, THEY WERE WITH YOU?

THEY'RE OKAY. THEY'RE COMING.

POP, I GOTTA TALK TO YOU.

I'LL JUST GO ON, MEET THE KIDS.

WHAT IS IT, SID?

I TOLD POP WHAT THE COPS MADE US DO AT THE GAME.

...AND THEN I WAS SUPPOSED TO GET IT BACK TO THE GUY, SO HE'D NEVER *SUSPECT*.

THIS *GUY*? WHO?

I DON'T KNOW. THEY SAID HE WAS A RED AGITATOR.

RED-- WHAT DID HE *LOOK* LIKE?

I DUNNO, POP. JUST A *GUY*, DRESSED REGULAR. BUT I SAW THE PAPER. IT WAS A LIST OF *NAMES*.

POP, *YOUR* NAME WAS ON IT. SO WAS *MRS. V.'S.*

AH.

THEY SNAPPED THE PHOTO. BUT THEN THE FIGHTING STARTED AND THE PHOTOGRAPHER GOT JUMPED.

I-- WE-- WE WRECKED THE CAMERA AND THE FILM.

AND THE LIST? WHERE'S THE LIST, SID? HAVE YOU GOT IT?

I HAD IT, BUT THIS DEVLIN FROM THE RED SQUAD TRIED TO SEARCH ME.

I SLIPPED IT INTO YOUR FRIEND'S POCKET AND TOLD THEM I DROPPED IT IN THE FIGHT.

WHAT FRIEND?

THE POLICEMAN. ALLISON, FROM THE ARMY.

HE WAS THERE, BUT NOT IN UNIFORM. THEN DEVLIN MADE HIM GO HELP LOOK FOR THE PAPER.

THE KITCHEN WAS STIFLING.

IF THE **RED SQUAD** GETS THAT LIST, THEY'LL MAKE TROUBLE FOR US. WE'LL LOSE OUR JOBS, SURE.

WHY?

EVERYONE ON THAT LIST IS TRYING TO ORGANIZE WORKERS FOR **BETTER PAY.** THE MAN THEY TOOK IT FROM HAS COME TO TOWN TO HELP US.

WE'RE THE "RADICALS." THEY'LL COME AFTER US FIRST. THEY THINK WE'LL START A REVOLUTION.

WILL YOU?

LET'S START WITH A DECENT WAGE AND A COFFEE BREAK.

MAYBE WE SHOULDN'T HAVE RISKED IT, TERESA. LOSING TWO WAGES IN THE SAME HOUSE...

WE ALL TAKE RISKS. THE REAL QUESTION IS, WHAT WILL BERT DO WHEN HE FINDS THE LIST?

BECAUSE HE WILL-- IF HE HASN'T ALREADY.

I'M SORRY. I DIDN'T KNOW WHAT ELSE TO DO. HE WAS THE CLOSEST ONE...

IT'S ALL RIGHT, SID. YOU DID THE BEST YOU COULD.

THIS BERT--

HE'S A GOOD MAN. YOU SAID IT YOURSELF JAKE, A MENSCH.

I KNOW, BUT HE'S ALSO A *COP*. WHAT WAS HE DOING THERE IN PLAINCLOTHES?

YOU THINK HE'S *SPYING*? RED SQUAD?

THEY COULD BE USING HIM BECAUSE HE KNOWS US. MAYBE *THAT'S* WHY HE WAS THERE AT THE STATION: THEY SUSPECTED US *ALREADY*.

NAW, *COME ON*! HE'S A *BEAT COP*. THAT'S HIS *NEIGHBOURHOOD*.

I THINK HE WAS HELPING US. HE SCARED A GUY OFF ME.

WE CAN'T TAKE THE CHANCE. I HAVE TO *FIND* HIM BEFORE SOMETHING HAPPENS. MAYBE I CAN--

YOU CAN *WHAT?*

I DON'T KNOW.

WANT ME TO COME?

BETTER NOT. SOMEBODY SHOULD BE HERE IN CASE THE RED SQUAD COMES FOR TERESA.

SID, YOU MIGHT GET YOUR WISH. WE'LL *BOTH* HAVE TO FIND WORK IF I GET FIRED.

WHAT THE HELL WE'LL WORK *AT*, I DON'T KNOW.

I'LL BE BACK AS SOON AS I--

I'M GOING *WITH YOU.*

NO, SID.

POP, I CAN HELP. I--

STOP! *LISTEN!*

SOMEONE'S COMING THIS WAY...

CLOP CLOP...

CLOP CLOP... CLOP...

KNOCK KNOCK KNOCK

IT'S **BERT**. BERT **ALLISON**. CAN I COME IN?

S-- SURE, BERT. C'MON IN.

GOOD EVENING. SORRY TO INTERRUPT.

NO PROBLEM. UH, BERT, THIS IS MY WIFE, **TERESA**. AND MY **FATHER**.

TERESA, PAPA, **BERT ALLISON**. I HEAR YOU **MET** THE KIDS.

A PLEASURE. HELLO, JAKE. **MISSUS, KIDS.** GLAD YOU'RE HOME SAFE.

THANKS FOR THAT, BERT.

THAT'S PARTLY WHY I CAME BY. WANTED TO MAKE SURE EVERYONE WAS OKAY.

IT'S NOT OVER UP THERE BY A **LONG SHOT**, BUT WE'LL GET IT SETTLED.

HAVE A SEAT, MR. ALLISON.

A **DRINK**?

NO, THANKS. CAN'T STAY.

THE **OTHER** REASON I CAME BY: ONE OF YOU DROPPED SOMETHING BACK THERE.

HERE, DID I--

YOU MEAN YOU FOUND THAT LI--

THE *PAPER* YOU WERE LOOKING FOR?

AH, *HERE* IT IS! THIS PACKET OF *SNAPSHOTS.* 'SCUSE ME FOR LOOKING, BUT I RECOGNIZED SOME OF YOU.

YOU GOT THE PHOTOS!

I'LL TELL YOU LATER.

THANK YOU, MR. ALLISON. I DIDN'T EVEN KNOW I *DROPPED* THEM.

WOOOOOOOOOOOOOOOOOOOOOOOOO...

SIRENS...

BUT DID YOU FIND *THE PAPER?*

WOooOooooooOooo

IT WAS MY DUTY TO BE THERE TONIGHT.

AS A *FATHER*, THAT IS. MY ELDEST BOY PLAYS LEFT FIELD FOR *ST. PETER'S*. HE HAD TWO HITS AND A RUN SCORED.

A *CHIP* OFF THE OLD *BLOCK*!

ARE THEY--

THEY'RE *SAFE*. THEY STUCK TOGETHER. THE TEAMS HAD NOTHING TO DO WITH IT.

IT'S A BUGHOUSE WORLD WHEN PEOPLE RIOT OVER A *BALL GAME*.

THAT'S NOT *ALL* THEY'RE FIGHTING OVER, IS IT?

NO, IT'S *NOT*. AND I DON'T KNOW WHICH MAKES ME SADDER.

GERMANY, WE *FIGHT* AGAIN, YOU SEE!

YOU'RE RIGHT. ONLY IT WON'T BE *US* FIGHTING. IT'LL BE OUR *CHILDREN*.

DON'T **SAY** THAT!

SORRY, MRS. VENDITELLI. DON'T MIND ME. THE **BOYS** HERE ALWAYS CALLED ME **CRAZY**.

BUT DID **YOU**--

IT'S BEEN A **WILD** NIGHT. IF YOU DON'T MIND, I'LL JUST GET A LIGHT FOR MY **PIPE** AND BE ON MY WAY.

FEDERICO, THE MATCHES!

DON'T **BOTHER**, SON.

...AND BOB'S YOUR UNCLE. I'M OFF.

BERT, *THANKS*. THE KIDS...

ENJOY THE PHOTOS. BE GOOD. *'NIGHT ALL!*

EVER READ *ASHES TO ASHES*, BY *BERNIE TUPP?*

I THINK WE JUST *DID*.

YOUR *SHOULDER?*

I'LL TELL YOU LATER. ROSIE SAVED ME.

WHY AM I NOT SURPRISED? AND YOU AND BERT SAVED US.

THIS CALLS FOR A *CELEBRATION*!

FEDERICO, GET THE GLASSES!

NONNO'S BEST, FOR THE OCCASION!

YOU WERE RIGHT, ANGELO. BERT IS A *MENSCH*. TO PEACE, TO FRIENDS.

SALUTI!

Epilogue

THE RIOT AT CHRISTIE PITS WENT ON TILL AFTER MIDNIGHT. THERE'S ONLY ONE PHOTO OF IT; YOU CAN'T SEE MUCH.

(IT'S TOO BAD ROSIE DIDN'T BRING HER CAMERA OR THERE MIGHT HAVE BEEN SOME GOOD ONES.)

IF ANYONE CAN WIN SOMETHING LIKE THAT, OUR CROWD DID. THEY TOOK A STAND AND DIDN'T BACK DOWN. FOR US, THAT WAS BIGGER THAN BAER BEATING SCHMELING.

WORD WAS, TOMMY HOPPED A FREIGHT OUT OF TOWN THAT SAME NIGHT. WE NEVER SAW HIM AGAIN.

POP AND TERESA KEPT THEIR JOBS. TERESA'S UNION LED A STRIKE IN 1935 THAT GOT A WAGE HIKE FOR WOMEN GARMENT WORKERS AND THE WORKWEEK REDUCED FROM FIFTY-FIVE HOURS TO FORTY.

BUT THE UNIONS ARGUED WITH EACH OTHER. POP GOT TIRED OF IT AND STARTED HELPING A NEW POLITICAL PARTY, THE CCF, INSTEAD.

MR. SHULMAN AT MARCELLE PHOTOGRAPHY STUDIO WAS SO IMPRESSED WITH ROSIE'S SNAPS THAT HE OFFERED TO APPRENTICE HER INTO THE BUSINESS.

SHE STARTED WORK THERE AND WENT TO HARBORD COLLEGIATE NIGHTS.

PLUG GOT WORK SINGING AND DOING ROUTINES TO ATTRACT FAIR GOERS TO THE HONEY DEW STAND AT THE CANADIAN NATIONAL EXHIBITION THAT YEAR.

EVERYBODY AGREED HE WAS BETTER AS A SOLO ACT.

WHEN HE GOT TO HARBORD, HE JOINED THE GLEE CLUB AND MET A COUPLE OF WISE GUYS NAMED JOHNNY WAYNE AND FRANK SHUSTER.

HARRY SUITCASE VANISHED IN 1936.
MOST OF HIM TURNED UP IN TORONTO
HARBOUR THE NEXT SPRING.

MAYOR STEWART GOT THE POLICE COMMISSION TO OUTLAW THE
SWASTIKA IN TORONTO. THAT DIDN'T MAKE IT HEAVEN, BUT IT HELPED.

HITLER KEPT ON PERSECUTING JEWS IN
GERMANY. EVEN *THE TELEGRAM* BEGAN
TO BELIEVE IT WAS SERIOUS.

ME? I FINALLY FOUND A PART-TIME JOB AT A BAKERY: DELIVERIES AND GENERAL HELP. IT PAID TWENTY-FIVE CENTS A WEEK AND ANY STALE BREAD I COULD TAKE HOME.

I STAYED IN SCHOOL, TOO. AFTER ALL THAT HAPPENED, I DECIDED I WANTED TO BE A LAWYER: A THINKING FIGHTER. WITH SENIOR FOURTH, HIGH SCHOOL, AND A YEAR WORKING TO MAKE TUITION, I FIGURED IT WOULD TAKE SIX YEARS FROM 1933 TO GET TO LAW SCHOOL.

BUT NONNO AND BERT WERE RIGHT. AND AS POP SOMETIMES SAID, *MAN TRACHT UN GOTT LACHT*, WHICH MEANS...

...MAN PLANS AND GOD LAUGHS.

Historical Note

The story of Sid, his family and his friends is made up, but it is set in places and events that were all too real. The year 1933 was the dark heart of the Great Depression. Farms and businesses failed. Factories closed. At least thirty workers in every hundred were jobless. There was no government "social safety net" to protect anyone. Many families endured poverty, eviction and breadlines. Homeless men "rode the rails" on freight trains, looking for work and sometimes begging.

In Germany, Adolf Hitler led his Nazi Party to victory in elections, unleashing a reign of terror on Jews and other groups. Canada was little more welcoming — unless immigrants were white, British and Protestant. The Canadian government's policy toward accepting others was later said to be "none is too many," even while newspapers carried reports from Germany about Nazi persecution.

Toronto, a much smaller city then, was not much better. Minorities were kept out of professions, neighbourhoods and even stores and vacation spots. Non-British people — mostly Jewish, with some Italians and a very few Black and Chinese families — clustered in the Ward, a poor downtown neighbourhood, and the Kensington area, just west. Those with jobs worked for low wages, mostly in garment factories, construction and manual labour. Those calling for unions and workers' rights were watched by the police. Chief Dennis Draper imagined violent revolutionaries behind every lamppost.

In the steamy summer of 1933, people from the Ward and Kensington went to beaches in the east end of the city for relief. There, residents fearful of "foreigners" organized neighbourhood patrols to keep them out. They called themselves swastika clubs and openly wore the symbol already made infamous by the Nazis. Trouble brewed in the heat. Confrontations followed, both there and in Willowvale Park, also known as Christie Pits, northwest of Kensington, where the notorious Pit Gang were just as dangerous to anyone they saw as an outsider.

Despite pleas for calm and denunciations of the swastika clubs by Mayor William Stewart, a riot erupted at a baseball diamond in Christie Pits on the evening of August 16, 1933, when a homemade swastika banner was unfurled during a softball game between the St. Peter's Church and Harbord Playground teams. The Harbord players were mostly Jewish. Word spread quickly beyond the park. Young men from Kensington and the Ward raced to the scene with whatever they could lay their hands on, to fight the Pit Gang.

The rioting lasted four hours. Many suspected the police were deliberately slow to respond because Chief Draper hoped the Jews and Italians would get a beating. The opposite happened instead.

The city was outraged. Mayor Stewart tried to have Draper fired, but the chief had too many powerful friends. Stewart did succeed in reaching out to the Jewish community, and in banning the swastika: anybody wearing one would be arrested.

The riot at Christie Pits became an early and potent symbol of immigrant pride and solidarity as the storm clouds of World War II slowly gathered. Nonetheless, it did not end the tradition of quiet bigotry against Jews and others in Canada.

Today, many things are different. The Nazis were defeated in World War II. Social services can help those who need them. Toronto has become an exciting and diverse major city, home to people from all around the world.

Still, when times are troubled, there can be a longing for simple answers to complicated problems. Often the easiest thing for some to do is blame anyone who seems "different": those who speak differently, worship differently, look or dress differently.

Sound familiar? The past of 1933 may be long ago and far away, but some of its darkness lurks with us still. That's why we made this book.

Acknowledgements

Many people have worked tirelessly to make this book possible. First and foremost, our thanks to the wonderful team at Scholastic Canada. Anne Shone (who believed, and got the ball rolling), Andrea Casault and Erin Haggett have somehow made it all make sense. Their vision, talents and patience were invaluable. Helping get it to you are Denise Anderson, Nikole Kritikos, Maral Maclagan and Cali Platek.

While any mistakes are ours, our thanks go to Frank Bialystok, University of Toronto, and Douglas Fyfe, for reading and commenting on our work. And we are grateful for research material from many sources, including: Breakthrough Entertainment, producers of *The Riot at Christie Pits* documentary film; the City of Toronto Archives; the Ontario Jewish Archives; *The Riot at Christie Pits*, by Cyril Levitt and William Shaffir; *Toronto Between the Wars: Life in the City 1919–1939,* by Charis Cotter; *Toronto Since 1918: An Illustrated History,* by James Lemon; *The Ward: The Life and Loss of Toronto's First Immigrant Neighbourhood,* by John Lorinc, Michael McClelland, Ellen Scheinberg and Tatum Taylor (eds.); *I Remember Sunnyside* and *Toronto City Life: Old and New,* by Mike Filey; and *The Jews of Toronto: A History to 1937,* by Stephen A. Speisman.

For help with Italian and Yiddish, we're grateful to Susan Buscemi and Diane Kerner. Amy Tompkins at the Transatlantic Agency made the complicated simple. Finally, thanks to everyone who keeps alive the story of August 16, 1933.

From Ted: My thanks first to my super-talented collaborator, Josh Rosen, whose pictures brought the story to life. Josh's skills and unwavering enthusiasm have made this project a joy ever since I pitched him a half-formed idea while walking a labyrinth in Lumsden, Saskatchewan. Again, I'm hugely indebted to everyone at Scholastic Canada and Transatlantic, named above, with special thanks to Anne,

Andrea and Erin. Their support with this and other projects has meant the world to me.

Finally, my thanks again to Margaret, for putting up with me in the Pits, and to my Staunton/Stewart family.

From Josh: Thanks to Ted, for dreaming up this idea in the first place. It's his vision that sparked all this, and I couldn't have asked for a better creative partner. Thanks to Anne, for her constant encouragement and thoughtful notes. Thanks to Andrea, for the phone calls and for pushing me to be bolder. Thanks to Erin for helping to bring it all home.

Thanks to Sarah, for the love and support, and for being a second set of eyes. And thanks to all my comics community, for being sources of inspiration, shoulders to cry on and comrades in the grind.

Margaret Heenan

Ted Staunton is the award-winning author of over forty books for young people, including *What Blows Up* in The Almost Epic Squad series, the picture book *Friends for Real*, illustrated by Ruth Ohi, and the non-fiction title *It Seemed Like a Good Idea . . . : Canadian Feats, Facts and Flubs,* co-written with his son, Will Staunton. Ted's novel *Who I'm Not* won the John Spray Mystery Award.

Sarah Teatero

Josh Rosen is a comic artist and illustrator, who lives in Toronto, not far from Christie Pits. When he's not making comics, he works in children's arts education, helping students over a wide range of ages find their own creative voices. *The Good Fight* is his first full graphic novel.